The Poetry Book Society
Anthology 1987/88

G000047693

The
Poetry Book Society
Anthology 1987/88

Edited with an Introduction by
GILLIAN CLARKE

Hutchinson
London   Melbourne   Auckland   Johannesburg

This edition first published in 1987 by Hutchinson Ltd, an imprint of
Century Hutchinson Ltd., Brookmount House, 62–65 Chandos Place, London
WC2N 4NW, and by the Poetry Book Society Ltd., 21 Earls Court Square,
London SW5

Century Hutchinson Australia (Pty) Ltd.,
PO Box 496, 16–22 Church Street, Hawthorn, Melbourne, Victoria 3122

Century Hutchinson New Zealand Ltd.,
PO Box 40–086, 32–34 View Road, Glenfield, Auckland, 10

Century Hutchinson South Africa (Pty) Ltd.,
PO Box 337, Bergvlei 2012, South Africa

Phototypeset in Linotron Times
by Rowland Phototypesetting Ltd.,
Bury St Edmunds, Suffolk
Printed and bound in Great Britain by
Anchor Brendon Ltd., Tiptree, Essex

British Library Cataloguing in Publication Data

The Poetry Book Society anthology 1987/88.
  1. English poetry – 20th century
  I. Clarke, Gillian   II. Poetry Book Society
  821'.914'08   PR1225

  ISBN 0-09-171051-0

Contents

vi

Introduction

Who would refuse the flattery of an invitation to edit an anthology of poetry? To gather fresh work from a number of favourite poets, to send away a package of typescripts and to have it back as a book is a job to relish. In a mood of power and responsibility each editor must imagine she will get it right this time, unlike all the others. On the Desert Island I want my selection of English Verse, not the one which leaves out my favourite Yeats, Hardy, Heaney or Thomas.

There are special difficulties and pleasures in the task of editing *The Poetry Book Society Anthology*, because it is unique in printing new and almost all unpublished verse. It reflects what poetry is saying now. This means that selection does not entail reams of careful reading or a refined memory for good poems. The editor invites up to 70 poets to contribute a poem, then waits for the post. How many can be expected to have a poem ready in the weeks between invitation and deadline? What if, when the poem arrives, it is not up to scratch? A poet will not thank an editor for printing a freshly-written poem that its author will later regret, wish to refine or abandon. How long dare one wait for submissions before sending letters off to those missed, or even forgotten, on the first list? Compiling the list is difficult and I, like other editors, have left out favourite poets. Some of my favourites left themselves out. Some did not reply. Some replied with regret that they had nothing ready. Others were abroad, or had moved, or forgot.

I remember hearing an Australian say that there is very little variation in accent over his vast continent, whereas in Britain ten miles is often distance enough to change a voice completely. This is audibly true. If geography and demography provide a barrier, a fold of land, a loop of river, a hill high enough or a social gulf deep enough to encircle a community, then experience, myth, tone and accent rest special to that tribe and place, and the poet's voice is shaded by that nuance. In this way Britain is vast, bigger than a great continent. I have tried to include in the list poets who, in various ways, voice some of the vastness.

Nervously I awaited the replies. Almost by return of post came R. S. Thomas' 'Mass for Hard Times', a powerful response to a bitter contemporary world, referring to Brecht, speaking to God, to the reader and to the future. Chance timing caught R. S. Thomas at his best, still drily observing in old age the ugliness and folly about us. He seems to me the only living poet who consistently addresses the hard facts of a fragile earth in the hands of fools and despots. It is a brave vision and essential reading. But such poetry would not do without the company of other poems. We need the praise poem, the witty poem, (though R. S. Thomas is one of the wittiest of voices), the lyric, the poetry of landscape, indoorscape, love, privacy, the voice of the city and the country, of the North and South of England and the Celtic nations of the British Isles, of men and of women.

Of women. There are twenty three this time. It's close to what you'd expect, given the percentage of the reading population who are women, and the numbers who read and write poetry. One of the most impressive collections of poetry I have read in the two years I have spent as selector for the Poetry Book Society was The Journey by Eavan Boland. She is missing from this anthology. She had no poem ready. Seamus Heaney, that word-magician, was in America and out of touch. Other fine books were the *Selected Poems* of Anne Stevenson, Carol Rumens and Elizabeth Jennings. All three are here with poems caught at the moment of composition, fine addenda to fine books. I enjoy the wit of U. A. Fanthorpe and her clever, fluent attention to a wide range of human things. Ken Smith's book *Wormwood* is out almost at the same time as the poem from that collection we print here. Blake Morrison's 'Back' is a flavour of his new work concerned with Northern roots and Northern language. Jeremy Hooker's is fresh from recent travels in Israel.

Whenever I consider there is enough poetry already and that there is neither rhyme nor reason for writing another verse, I recall that Shakespeare and Emily Dickinson never saw snow in the headlamps of a car, never flew in a plane, watched a distant war on television or saw Saturn by satellite camera. The contact lens and the nuclear power station give a current language and imagery to work into verse. We must go on with it.

Gillian Clarke

THE POETRY BOOK SOCIETY
ANTHOLOGY 1987/88

DANNIE ABSE

In Jerusalem

Like walking through a perfume factory
with attar of rose, macerated violet,
oil of jasmine, censored by a heavy cold.

Or far from home, the language double-dutch,
the room a riot of open mouths. 'What? What?'
All laughing at a joke except yourself.

That aurulent Fall in Washington, remember,
at the National Gallery? A blind girl
with her blond fiancé facing a Monet.

Outside Vienna, they said to Beethoven,
'Charming, don't you agree, those distant cowbells?'
Suddenly, he wept. They thought, 'These musicians . . .'

Thirty years ago, in the ward, the hunchback
with syringomyelia. He could not feel
the lit cigarette smouldering his forearm.

Now here I am, motionless as a question-mark,
while each bearded man in tasselled shawl
hums and sways. The exclusivity of prayer!

If it is a prayer and not an orgy where
all – such busy cries and torment – fornicate
with holy spirits against a wall.

DANNIE ABSE

Smiling Through

All great art is praise.   John Ruskin

I
Then there's the parable of three wise men
(always three, as in a joke), who walk
in their fresh linen through the sweet morning
till they hear fat busy flies, see a dog,
stiff legs in the air, disintegrating.
'What a terrible sight!' cries the first beard.
'What a terrible smell!' complains the second.
'What lovely white teeth,' the third, rapturously.

II
The scandalous paradox of cripples
and slums in a world of colours.

Praise the white tooth.

The expensive bombs blessed with holy cries
falling on the screams of mothers.

Praise the white tooth.

III
Meanwhile, sky in narrow streets;
yet turning the hands of a clock,
as one might do at bedtime
(though it is only afternoon)
something may fall away or arrive:
another place, a beautiful
virus-free clearing where, of course,
everybody is so happy
not least the three up-market shepherds
everything grassy and bird-song,
flower-pretty and river sound,
the sky blue blue blue everywhere
over this landscape waiting for
a Poussin. But look – in the dark
green shadow of that light green tree
a human skull, teeth in its jaw
uttering, 'I, too, am in Arcady.'

IV
The famine babies with ponderous eyes
in a careless world of plenty.

Praise the white tooth.

The future with Chernobyl disease
in one year or in twenty?

Praise the white tooth.
Praise the white tooth.

FLEUR ADCOCK

Wildlife

A wall of snuffling snouts in close-up,
ten coloured, two in black and white,
each in its frame; all magnified,
some more than others. Voles, are they?
Shrews? Water-rats? Whiskers waggling,
they peep from under twelve tree-roots
and vanish. Next, a dozen barn owls,
pale masks, almost filling the dark screens.
Cut; and now two dozen hedgehogs
come trotting forward in headlong pairs:
they'll fall right out on the floor among the
cookers and vacuum-cleaners unless
the camera – just in time – draws back.
Here they come again, in their various
sizes, on their various grass:
olive, emerald, acid, bluish,
dun-tinged, or monochrome. The tones
are best, perhaps, on the 22-inch
ITT Squareline: more natural
than the Philips – unless you find them too
muted, in which case the Sony
might do. Now here are the owls again.

Meanwhile at the Conference Centre
three fire-engines have screamed up. Not,
for once, a student smoking in a bedroom:
this time a cloud of thunderflies
has chosen to swarm on the pearly-pink
just-warm globe of a smoke-detector.

PATRICIA BEER

My Neighbour's Geese

December is the nimble month for my neighbour's geese.
Their field is higher than my window.
All year I look up at them
Fighting on the spot
Eating round their feet.
Winter is their prime and they move.

Through the patchy frost, one foot crackling one silent
They break out of their frame.
A lightweight I carried back up the hill
His beak rubbing
Against my jaw. My neighbour
Was already ill and could not rejoice.

Geese once cackled in Rome like guardian angels
And stood for something in fairy tales
Far away from Devon. December
Seems to remind them.
Along the lane they go
Straining forward like figureheads on ships.

This December, grey in an ashen afternoon,
They materialized in our courtyard
Ships no longer, more like stray dogs
Anxious and blurred.
I found my neighbour
Who said 'Not mine. The fox got mine.'

They were not doppelgängers or ghosts, nor the fox's
Who eats up the last movement.
They were his. But he was sitting
In a hard chair stock-still
Watching his father's farm stir,
And roll like Jordan into the Dead Sea.

JAMES BERRY

Spirits of Movement

Surely, so alike, airborne wind gave birth
to water, issued the denser wash
and earthed the early offspring.

Inbuilt is wind-inheritance.
Rage of leaves resists face-wash
its wind's arrival in trees.

Hear sea waves work-choir,
hear any waterfall wonder,
its temple-roar of wind flooding woods.

A restless transparent busyness
going and going, spirits of movement,
both break all shores, mad-mad in search.

Wind plays wild bands of ghosts.
Water organizes running river
and drives rain-floods hustling.

On any sitting duty
like being a pond or puddle,
canal or glassful

water waits to run away
or just disappear like wind.
In a settled state water is sad.

Drop a stone in a sleepy pool
you hear the sulk
of static water voiced.

Lock up water, give it time, it'll leave.
Drink it down, it presses wanting exit.
A job done, water vanishes.

Water'll freshen any body part
and be ready, hanging
in drips, to be off.

Does it work, yes. But to be
ungraspable, like wind,
water insists on its transfiguration.

JAMES BERRY

Black Kid in a New Place

I'm here, I see
I make a part of a little planet
here, with some of everybody now.

I stretch myself, I see
I'm like a migrant bird
who will not return from here.

I shake out colourful wings.
I set up a palmtree bluesky
here, where winter mists were.

Using what time tucked in me, I see
my body pops with dance.
Streets break out in carnival.

Rooms echo my voice. I see
I was not a migrant bird. I am
a transplanted sapling, here, blossoming.

ALISON BRACKENBURY

Temperature

My head's the axis. I am turning, turning.
My feet make a compass through starry water.
The sun is spinning inside my eyes.

'Are you going to die?' asks my daughter, robed
On the hairdresser's stool in a long rose gown.
Gravely she watches dark hair snipped down.

My eyes are the axis, turning, turning.
The sun is spinning, like you, my daughter.
Out of the compass of my head
My feet are crossing the starry water.

ALISON BRACKENBURY

The Lane

I do not remember the name of the lane.
Bent like a dog's hind leg, it ran
Behind two villages; at the joint came
To a concrete bungalow where a thin dog
Danced on its chain, where sometimes a man
Called it off, rough as a voice through the fog.

Caudell? Northfield? Somersby? No.
I can say, at the far end, rose a wood
Whose violets crept through pine-needles, so
Short-stemmed it was hard to pick them. Then
Came the sudden hill, where my legs and heart stood
As they burst; to the clank of a bicycle chain.

I should not have gone there alone; and yet
The only place where I stood afraid
Was the emptied cottage, where the wet
Rose scrambled nettles; where inside
Faint flowers left mould; beyond, the pond;
In which I thought some miracle must hide.

Only young rabbits appeared, scenting dusk,
Who were not certain if they were afraid,
Sat frozen for long breaths; then gave me up.
They flicked fringed ears, then turned back instead
To untrodden grass, to red bramble-leaves, played
In glimmered hedge-tunnels, nodding their heads.

After belonging, I strained to go free.
I have seen tawny foxes, springing down walls,
Met the owl's wide stare in the winter tree.
Only in sleep, I pass down there again,
Hear the dog's chain sink, the rabbits' feet pause,
The light stems snap – You walked with me there, once.
Do you remember the name of the lane?

ALAN BROWNJOHN

Sea Pieces

I
Coming in here from the saloon where friends
Are smiling across at each other, she gives
This worried look to herself in the mirror,
And goes hard at the problem of her hair,
The sun having had her face and her hair being fraught,
Or tight, or clenched by even the delicate
Attentions of the breeze, with a honey-coloured
Comb. Why descend now to the cabin, the decks are full
Of the kindest smiles? A calm sea sways her
Easily on the autumn boat, she shifts without
Thinking in the pitch of it, half of her relaxed
And serene with her waters, liking the spray
Which rinses her window, but half of her fraught.
A man is bicycling along the sand,

II
Choosing the firmest places, where his wheels
Will not sink far. He listens to their hiss
With only the sea on his right, the waves pushing
Regularly towards him and very small.
He arrived here down a lane where September offers
All colours of a blackberry at once,
And at the dunes he carries his vehicle
Over gorse and over dry sand and at the sea
Sets it down facing westward in the so-profound
Late afternoon light. He mounts and pedals off
As he notices the boat far out, its portholes,
Its smoke, but not the woman in her cabin
Combing her hair cut with a serious stare.
Coal is unloading at a small quay,

III

Exactly . . . *there*. Oh I see where you mean,
That little port the boat is passing, an old tub
Unloading an irregular cargo of sea-coal
In rumbling quantities, or screes, in shifting
Mouths debouching on innocent land
As it stirs in the waters, tethered to the quay?
This coal, they say, has come from Germany,
Unloading in the so-serene late sun,
Which is day by day the more impermeable
To the onset of autumn, much as the woman's hair
For a time deters the distractions of her comb.
She drags at it and frowns, she tugs the knots
Apart, so the strands can flow and the ship move,
And the leaves tug from the trees, and the pedals turn.

ALAN BROWNJOHN

April Light

Slowly the tree falls, and we lean back
On our axes watching it, in the film,
Leaning on arm-rests in the Odeon.
The trunk and riven stump will kill nobody
In the real April daylight we had then.
So when the man with the name my friend had
Thirty years ago, and a credible address,
Dies today in the *Guardian*, struck by a falling tree,
This is fiction, it can't *be* him, it's a common name,
And trees fall commonly in reported storms.
So I don't go to the telephone, and I don't start
To write at last the letter I never wrote
When neglect was slowly cutting away at friendship.
I laugh at the idea, at the superstition,
And lean back in my chair, watching the light
Fall on a spring day killingly like winter.

CHARLES CAUSLEY

Family Feeling

My Uncle Alfred had the terrible temper.
Wrapped himself up in its invisible cloak.
When the mood was on his children crept from the kitchen.
It might have been mined. Not even the budgie spoke.

He was killed in the First World War in Mesopotamia.
His widow rejoiced, though she never wished him dead.
After three years a postcard arrived from Southampton.
'Coming home Tuesday. Alf,' was what it said.

His favourite flower he called the antimirrhinum.
Grew it instead of greens on the garden plot.
Didn't care much for children, though father of seven.
Owned in his lifetime nine dogs all called Spot.

At Carnival time he rode the milkman's pony.
Son of the Sheikh, a rifle across his knee.
Alf the joiner as Peary in cotton-wool snowstorms.
Secret in cocoa and feathers, an Indian Cree.

I recognized him once as the Shah of Persia.
My Auntie's front-room curtains gave him away.
'It's Uncle Alf!' I said, but his glance was granite.
'Mind your own business, nosey,' I heard him say.

I never knew just what it was that bugged him,
Or what kind of love a father's love could be.
One by one his children bailed out of the homestead.
'You were too young when yours died,' they explained to me.

Today, walking through St Cyprian's Church-yard
I saw where he lay in a box the dry colour of bone.
The grass was tamed and trimmed as if for a Sunday.
Seven antimirrhinums in a jar of stone.

ANTHONY CONRAN

At Dolwyddelan

I hear them call, '. . . wedi marw' –
Up to the high keep on the hill.
Llywelyn dead in the south.
I look down through the watcher's eyes.

Through this arrow chink
Consternation of centuries
Is jagged as fork lightning.
I stare with the eyes of a young boy.

The terror of death, dreariness
Of all my own deaths, my father's
Heart rasping to a close, Vic Neep
Daubing till the tumours dried his mind;

Paul Nicholson, daring us to die for him,
The vortex of his threat
Savaging us –
Then jumping to the rocks from Menai Bridge;

Mike, downed in a car crash at night;
Linda in whom light lived, but cancer killed;
And now to the fruiting of snowdrops
Eirlys, the vivid, dies.

My sight shrivels. I turn to run.
Dreariness reaching back.
Procession of all my friends
Into that cry in the dawn –

The procession of my people
Calling up to me for seven centuries
As the Cilmeri raven
Wheels on the wing towards Dafydd in Dolbadarn.

DAVID CONSTANTINE

Mistress

Women whose hands know the feel of a baby's head
Push them confidently in among the melons
And their strong brown thumbs side by side,
Beautifully cuticled, feel for give on the crown.

That summer of the hot winds and the fires
The melons were sold split. He held me one
Before we had paid for it, before all the people,
To smell the inside of at its small
Opening fleur-de-lys and we went down
In a river of laughter between the banked stalls
Among all the people swinging our fruit in a net.

He made the cuts but I opened it
And for a moment my hands were a bowl of flames.
I served him cradles and the moons of nursery rhymes
And a family of rocking boats. We ate
And our mouths ran over with luscious smiles.

Then he closed my hands into a fist and held them shut.

DAVID CONSTANTINE

Martyr

This man, if we can call him that, this foetus,
This white larva, he was there at the Dry Tree
As a merry child, a pig-minder, when Christ,
So we believe, (the dates do tally) did that
Trick with spittle and two dead eyes and the sight
Or was it the ensuing loud hallelujah
Or being spotted in the stinking mayweed
Tugging away at himself no doubt among
Our burned-out necklaces and the handy stones
And Jesus telling him to cross his heart and
Hope to die if he told a soul about it
(Everyone did) and him telling his mam? It
Blew the wits of that doughty little witness
Of many occurrences on that bloody spot.
His mam never saw the stars of his eyes again.
She watched him curl and eavesdropped on his nightmares.
She even petitioned the travelling Master
To please come and wipe her little man's vision
Clean of the miracle. We reckon in his fist
(Observe how over the years he has eaten at it)
We'll find the crooked sixpence Jesus flicked him
When our blind brother saw the heavenly blue.

IAIN CRICHTON SMITH

The Cat

You were eighty-five when the cat appeared
one night at your door. It was perfectly white.
You wouldn't let it into the house but you fed it
on scraps of fish which you placed on a blue plate.
It reared at your bedroom window like a stoat
mewing to get in: but you refused.
Sometimes you would threaten it with your fist.
What a strange white bony animal it was.
It would stare at you intently from the grass
and you would think: This thin beast troubles me.
My bones too are shaken as if he
were a sinister part of me, that had gone
hunting inquisitively about the stones.
The night before you died it stared fiercely
in through the window, a tall vertical eel.
Its concentration was unshakeable.
And your bones melted and you lay at last,
a plate beside you, while your stubbly beard
had a fishy tang, wild, perilous, abhorred.

IAIN CRICHTON SMITH

Snow

Snow, you create a country of ghosts.
To you perhaps our souls might migrate,
you are the land of the souls that confronts us,
seeming eternal yet of course not so.

We rise in the morning to shrouded trees,
to houses with fairy tale windows,
to hills voluminous and novel,
to a fresh country without signposts.
This silence, where does it come from?
This holy quietness.
This blankness without the individual,
this communal burial.

Magician, you have cast your handkerchief over us.
We are lost in the folds.
We struggle to find the road again
Where is our destination?

Or shall we holiday in childhood
with our red gloves and jumpers
plunging up to our waists
in the gravity of the adult.

Or as in a mirror do we see our souls
so whitely staring back at us
with a conspicuous sparkle,
the doubleness of death.

Yet it is not so, it is not eternal.
Suddenly the hills become water,
the fragile windows are cracked
and the green land appears
somehow stagy and distant:
after that soul-knowledge
the body with its smells and veins,
our undisguisable home.

KEVIN CROSSLEY-HOLLAND

Above the Spring Line

in celebration of the Ridgeway

I
Under the moon's pale razor
under the warm eye
under the chamber of clouds
under rain-dance and hail-bounce

in this latitude of shadows

blazing the green limbs
foot-friend and far-reacher
master of compounds

II
Overseer of Epona and the fleet horses at Lambourn
the bigwigs in their hill-stations at Silbury and Chequers

keeper of Dragon Hill and the craters on the bombing range
also the quaking grass the brome grass melilot and eyebright

warden of the Og and the watercress beds and Goring Gap
the sarsens like dowdy sheep and the dowdy sheep like
                                        sarsens

custodian of the downs and brakes the strip lynchets and
                                        warrens
under the lapwing the glider's wing spring of yellowhammers

III
And spring is the word. I can almost forget
yesterday – the sweat stain semen stain smudge
of chalk and in the hedge the sodden butts
the jagged bottle and a bloodstained rag

Here are wiry snowdrops bedded in beech mast
where wild pigs rooted. *Fuses* everywhere
The spindle and bryony shrug their shoulders
Birch-twigs pinken, generations within

IV
A man laps at a dewpond, lays his hoar-head on his knapsack
knobby with Brandon flint. A girl in a mauve shift bares her
                                                                        throat
Trials riders tight-lipped burn through crimson and purple
                                                                        rosettes

A crocodile of the literal-minded steamy and singing
I will lift up mine eyes set their sights on the escarpment

Ah! the drover sleeps in a butterfly wimple – chalk-hill blues
flutter in and out of his mouth and here above the spring line
a hunter smiles as he snares such a pretty Chiltern gentian

V
It is all within me
written in chalk, and written
in your hand it is yours

whatever you may also choose . . .

From Overton to Ivinghoe
sunlight and ribs of shadow
pressing behind us and coursing
through us. We are conductors

TONY CURTIS

At Ochrid Lake

for Zoran Anchevsky

After the monastery of Sveta Naum,
after the frescoes and the blank spaces
of the stolen frescoes,
after the poems and cameras
and the sound-crew man who played for us
James Taylor on his guitar, we swim
beneath the mountains
in the lake's shallow warmth,
feet curling over the smooth, muddy pebbles.

Around the headland Albania's
border-posts, visa checks, the guard's cold eyes.
Across the lake are the blue-distant Greek hills.
Macedonia wedged into the Balkans –
tyrannized, subjugated, partitioned
by Greeks, Serbs, Bulgars, Turks, Nazis,
the Austro-Hungarian Empire,
century after century.

Zoran, once you climbed in these mountains
to find still the scars of the Great War –
shallow trenches cut into the rocks,
brambles of wire, shells, skulls
bleached white like great birds' eggs.

Beneath the hills
from the shadowed groves at our backs
pure water springs from the ground,
gathers into a river that courses
a current clear through the lake.

As we wade from the shallows
further into the flow, the river hits
us like a wall of cold. Suddenly
icy the water's caress turns
to manacles locked around our legs –
it is like the promise of death, then
under this faultless sky,
like death itself.

TONY CURTIS

Driving West

each time I stop here
with flowers, a trowel, springtime bulbs,
but now the heel of my shoe fails
to mark the grave's solid earth.

On this brightest of February days
the flowers are bruised and wasted,
fisted out of the vase by its stale
water clenched into ice.
For the church has thrown a shadowed pall
over the graveyard's north-west.

After tea my mother keeps off the t.v.
and talks of her own grave.
I know how you felt about Dad's cremation.
I thought of asking the chapel at Jameston.
You would come down and look after me,
wouldn't you? You always call at Gran's.

I should rise and take her in my arms,
but joke my assent, instead.
So many chances missed, so many failings
when warmth should force beginnings.

When I phoned Glangwili late at night
the nurse re-assured me – yes, the morning
would be early enough.
                    Your grandmother?
She's sleeping now, all right?
There's no immediate danger.

These past nine years,
each drive west I stop
and tend her grave. Small recompense
for that night's troubled sleep,
the last words left unsaid.
Dying alone must be like this
driving into the rapid, chilling dusk
and knowing yourself lost.

MAURA DOOLEY

Shadow on Her Desk

A year after the courtroom heard those tapes
I'm running through the dark blue evening,
October fires keen on the wind, winter quickening.

In the tightening of fingers and the tightening of rules
something terrible was being hidden from us,
only the fear passed on, in rumour, safe at school.

Never take sweets from strangers (I'm running).
Don't accept lifts from people you don't know.
Better to be safe than sorry (I'm running).

That Friday I burst into a house doused with fish
my mother busy cooking, my father shushing me,
full of all my news my father shuts me up.

But I am shut before he says it,
seeing him crying, staring at the telly, crying.
Coal that burns in our grate has shut them up.

A slag heap, a tip, a shadow on her desk,
safe at school it shut them in the ground.
Safe at school it shut them.

After twenty years the one they tugged clear
stares out beyond the whirr of cameras to
the valley. Children gone, work gone,

only the green and the rain keep returning.
Fir trees are planted on manmade hills,
they've put up a memorial in pale cement.

After twenty years we are raking over old coals
but something terrible is being hidden from us,
only the fear passed on, in rumour, safe at school.

Don't play outside today (I'm crying).
Wash all green-leafed vegetables thoroughly.
Don't drink rainwater (I'm crying).

Saddleworth, Aberfan, Chernobyl: a kind of litany.
Up on the wet green moor police start to dig.

MAURA DOOLEY

Developing a Passion

It used to be syphons and corks, a must,
A nose, stains in the linen cupboard,
A large red bucket, a deep red wine.
Now, the bathroom window blanketed,
Newspaper stuffing the door black shut,
Even his ears are plugged against day
And Mozart drowns her kitchen calls.
A room all dozy rose from a safety
Light constant as the North star,
A beacon, the presence of Christ.

'Do you want a drink?' she shouts.

His fingers puddle in search of images,
Paper darkens, chemicals blush,
Little miracles break out again and again.

'I'm leaving your glass here' she says.

He is busy with the loaves and fishes,
Forgetting wine, squinting at a reversed face,
Light spills over the darkness, over and over.

'How much longer are you going to be?'

Her voice has an urgency he cuts with
A spinning tap. Water will sluice each flaw,
Rinse away imperfection, fix truth for ever.

'I won't be long' he is calling.

Downstairs she has emptied the bottle,
Is weeping over a creased Polyfoto,
Is burning the Man Ray, the Bailey, the Brandt.

CAROL ANN DUFFY

Practising Being Dead

Your own ghost, you stand in dark rain
and light aches out from the windows
to lie in pools at your feet. This is the place.
Those are the big oak doors. Behind them
a waxed floor stretches away, backwards
down a corridor of years. The trees sigh.
You are both watching and remembering. Neither.

Inside, the past is the scent of candles the moment
they go out. You saw her, ancient and yellow,
laid out inside that alcove at the stairhead,
a broken string of water on her brow.
For weeks the game was Practising Being Dead,
hands in the praying position, eyes closed, lips
pressed to the colour of sellotape over the breath.

It is accidental and unbearable to recall that time,
neither bitter nor sweet but gone, the future
already lost as you open door after door, each one
peeling back a sepia room empty of promise.
This evening the sky has not room enough
to give you a shadow. Nobody hears
your footsteps walking away along the gravel drive.

HELEN DUNMORE

Dublin, 1971

The grass looks different in another country.
By a shade more or a shade less, it startles
as love does in the sharply-tinged landscape
of sixteen to eighteen. When it is burnt
midsummer and lovers have learned to make love
with scarcely a word said, then they see nothing
but what is closest: an eyelash tonight,
the slow spread of a sweat-stain,
the shoe-sole of the other as he walks off
watched from the mattress.

The top deck of the bus babels with diplomats'
children returning from school, their language
an overcast August sky which can't clear.
Each syllable melting to static
troubles the ears of strangers, no stranger
but less sure than the slick-limbed children.
With one silvery, tarnishing ring between them
they walk barefoot past the Martello tower
at Sandymount, and wish the sea clearer,
the sun for once dazzling, unfledged
from its wet summer nest of cloud strips.

They make cakes of apple-peel and arrowroot
and hear the shrieks of bold bad seven-year-old Seamus
who holds the pavement till gone midnight
for all his mother's forlorn calling.
The freedom of no-one related for thousands of miles,
the ferry forever going backward and forward
from rain runnel to drain cover . . .

The grass looks different in another country,
sudden and fresh, waving, unfurling
the last morning they see it as they go down
to grey Dun Laoghaire by taxi.
They watch the slate rain coming in eastward
pleating the sea not swum in,
blotting the Ballsbridge house with its soft sheets
put out in the air to sweeten.

DOUGLAS DUNN

The People Before

I've turned my back on Tuesday's half-past four
As 1985's obscured momentum
Falters towards the closing of an epoch.
Crepuscular, two tradesmen walking home
Know that they're woodcuts by a local master,
Firm local lines, modernity unstuck.

Migrating geese, in an upended V,
Caricature my watch's measurement,
Half-past the hour and continuity
In sepia, any time but now in this
Post-dated country etched in aquatint
Nearing the day of luck and all good wishes.

Streetlamps come on.
Frockcoated decades trespass on the tense.
Spent eras stain
Anachronistic stone –
Luminous echoes, gaslit reminiscence,
Distorted, thinned, Victorian.

A push can coax our gate
Into releasing an Edwardian squeak.
December's frozen rose
Nods to unseen applause
As a sparrow wings its startled featherweight
And petals tumble in a cruel slapstick.

Preliminary moonlight on the Firth
Casts in-betweenness on the time and light –
Not now, not then, not day, not night,
But moonlight's childhood, waterworn,
And, in one moment, all death, all birth,
All dying and being reborn.

Beyond our neighbours' frosted washing-lines,
Their silvered slates and chimneypots,
Our borderland begins
And light withdraws to loss of Monifieth,
Subplots and counterplots
Narrated in the coastline's myth.

Make what you can of it, for no one knows
What story's told by winter-misted hills
Or how a river flows
Against the tide in white scribbles.
A patiently daemonic frost
Sharpens its needles on the eastern coast.

Processionals of lives go by
On delicate, crisp treads,
Blurred fragrances, gently percussive,
Nimble over the unswept leaves.
Top-hatted heads of firms and kitchenmaids
Visit the instincts of the eye.

Swish, hush and microsound, the whispered *ahs*
Converse with silence's midpoint
Over the Firth, and time is disobedient,
Mixing its years and generations.
It's 1940 on the weatherglass
And now and then in the events of nations.

The night fills up with navigation's stars
Honed to a masterpiece of quiet.
Dismantled commerce hungers for its jute,
Esparto, timber, coal and mariners,
Prosperity and credit.
Lighthouses warn the swimmers on a lost trade route.

A candleflame, held by a child
Walking past, reddens a window, her face
A spectral captive in the window's glass,
Her neck a ruff of fiery nightgown lace.
Coniferous estates, the winterfield,
Submerge their farms in foliage and grass.

I turn a blacksmithed key in its lock;
The house of us now, love, of you and me.
More geese rant westward, flock by chevroned flock.
Feeling its freezing metal on their hands,
These other people turned this iron key;
The lunar honey fell on Buddon Sands.

JEAN EARLE

Eating a Pear

Passing through –
All winter to go before you call again –
You left me a pear from your garden
Fruitful between the weeds.
'Eat it now,' you advised.
'It's ready.'

I eat for the snows to come,
The dark days.

Slip by slip, off a silver knife . . .

Recalling your house
With the wood stove and the dried flowers
Echoing summer's colours. Your friends stand
Crowded against the light.
I cannot see
How far down your wild garden
Grows that tree which dropped
The pear you left me.

Darkness falls.
I hold the knife like pain.

JEAN EARLE

Up in the Great Oak

Boy's voice
Chanting obscenities
Inside the territory of this oak –
Against your bursts of noise
An oak is immortal.

Crown overhang
Pegs down perimeters
Structured like dinosaur's ribs
Or a king's house
From which you monkey-dangle,
Bellowing your noise.

An acorn falls . . .

Your smut shrills
Over the spent of twigs,
Fungi, shadows –
Stirs up delicate flies
That go down with the sun.
The other boys give up,
You shout on . . .

But now, in autumn,
The Green Man
Haunts this circuit
In a bush for priest-cloak,
Tracking your potent zest.

He does as he must
For life's renewal.
You – crude voice –
Young Adonis, Osiris,
The nourishing Christ.

JEAN EARLE

Still Life

There was a child born dead.
Time has bleached out the shocking insult,
Ageing has cicatrized the body's wound . . .

Still I do not like to prune bushes
That push to the sun –
Nor put my broom into the spider's house
Where she keeps her children
Many-legged, darting with terrible life.

Stern and efficient I peel potatoes
Sprouting intently in a dark bag.

Furtive, I slip one into the earth.
'Grow!' I say. 'Grow, if you must . . .'

CHRISTINE EVANS

Proving

for Anne Stevenson and the Poetry Bookshop, Hay-On-Wye

Some days, like this one
when I got your book
slide by too quickly. There's a feeding
stillness where I am, inside,
but real mealtimes
thicken on the skyline, soundlessly zoom up
blocking the light
like weather watched on time-lapse film.

The sky's a cleaner blue
than summer and the garden
beckons with sharp green. Wind and sun –
my white sheets hanker to be ocean-going
so I must keep on running out wide-armed
to gather them
and pin them safely back. And I have to keep
a weather eye on watch for any ewe
that might be choosing *soon* to heave her lambs
out into daylight. Three so far I've seen
pawing the ground, sky-pointing,
in oval nests they've turned of their own smell.
Worst, before the postman knocked, I'd set
a flour/yeast/water spell to work:
now kneading bread's last thing I want
or warm flesh either. My mind's alive
with words, your words, and leavened by them, mine
that will keep springing, sending shoots
in answer. Most of my days are tuned
to turning soil or gathering, but when
the stir of knowing and the soft
implosive bruise
of germination and the wind and sun
of carrying coincide, oh then

just give me time
and I might catch my breath and make such shapes
to prove and set and go on nourishing
longer, as amazingly, as bread.

CHRISTINE EVANS

Lucy's Bones

Most of our bodies will melt
letting all they ever were leak out.
Between the fires and the fresh ruins
folds of white fat
hiss and gutter till flesh flows.
But her bones will arch in the earth
not gently flexed as if in sleep
but sound as boat-staves, seasoned
timber that takes two generations to give way.

Mole-mouthed as a lover
rot will move over her
a charge of blue seed
quivering her skin, flooding
the packed, bright silks and the slit reefs,
prying under fingernails
disentangling white stalks
for the petals to fall free
and alchemize to a stencil.

Then her long bones
will be galleries of sighing
her ribcage a cathedral.
The wings of her shoulderblades
go on promising horizons, her pelvis
still pauses at the edge of its question.
The little carpal and the tarsal bones
lie orderly, arranged like pieces
waiting to clatter into prophecy.

The egg of her skull shall brim with honey.
In each eye-cave, a chrysalis
stir towards the shrouded sun.
Ladybird and velvet mite and dung beetle
seedpearls of snails' eggs
nest in the sockets of her knuckles.
In each dry crack, a patient germ.
White roots of fern and equisetum
already weave themselves a launch pad.

Her bones should be lodged in topmost branches
stirred at the heart of her own green storm
but her smile will shine out
through blinded ground, through deafened wind
because she stayed hungry all her life
kept her face to the edge
constantly spending
and was charged with such brightness
waste cannot claim her.

U. A. FANTHORPE

Friends' Meeting House, Frenchay

When the doors of the house are shut,
Eyes lidded, mouth closed, nose and ears
Doing their best to idle, fingers allowed out
Only on parole; when the lovely holy distractions,
Safe scaffolding of much-loved formulae,
Have been rubbed away; then the plant
Begins to grow. It is hard to rear,
Rare herb of silence, through which the Word comes.
Three centuries of reticent, meticulous lives
Have naturalized it on this ground.

And the herb is the Vine, savage marauder,
That spreads and climbs unstoppably,
Filling the house, the people, with massing insistent shoots
That leaf through windows and doors, that rocket through
                                    chimneys,
Till flesh melts into walking forms of green,
Trained to the wildness of Vine, which exacts
Such difficult witness; whose work is done
In hopeless places, prisons, workhouses,
In countinghouses of respectable merchants,
In barracks, collieries, sweatshops, in hovels
Of driven and desperate men.
                          It begins here
In the ground of silence.

U. A. FANTHORPE

Eating Out

Adventures into rehearsed but unknown living,
Table napkin tucked conscientiously under chin.

Choice of cutlery supervised, menu explained.
So much good behaviour was indigestible;

Mother took me outside to recover. Later,
Father introduced London cuisine:

How to handle moules marinières, not
To eat all the petits fours, or pocket them for later.

When the proper time came, he initiated me
Into the ritual consumption of lobster.

My last outing with him: teacakes in
A Petworth teashop. He leaned heavy on my arm,

But did the ordering. Mother died older, later;
I never accustomed myself to this autocrat's

Humble *I'll have whatever you're having, dear.*

JEREMY HOOKER

Walking to Capernaum

I
Such violence struck here –
a new thing, a word with power:

And thou, Capernaum,
which art exalted unto heaven,
shalt be brought down to hell.

A gentler word
where the sea laps the shore:
The damsel is not dead, but sleepeth.

II
What I feel most is the heat,
and sick at the unreality
of bad art:

a sloppy English poem
which someone has fixed on a wall
at the site of the miracle
of loaves and fishes;

new stained glass daubing
the interior of the chapel built
over the rock where Christ
is said to have said to Peter . . .

Compared to these,
I could love the wooden donkeys
and camels and holy families
from the factory at Bethlehem.

Unreal, in a sweat of heat
and bad blood, I dip
my seamy face in the water.

It tastes of salt, and is
a dull silvery blue
on a day of desert cloud.

A crane – not, thank God,
a symbol – but a white crane,
with long, wispy hairs at the back
of its neck, stands
fishing in the shallows.
A black lizard looks at me
over the edge of a black stone.

III
On the road between
orchards and tomato fields;
in the dust thrown up
by tourist coaches;
between the columns,
and among pine needles lying
on the ruins of Peter's house,
I try to imagine them:

the girl waking surprised,
with hunger in her eyes;
the woman cured by a touch;
that loud cry, the man
on the floor of the synagogue –
torn and empty, but clean.

What had he seen? What thing
had cried with his voice?

And the fishermen
as they put out –
from this moment, no
denial will swerve their aim.

The port they left behind
is a heap of blackened stone.

IV

It is evening, and very still;
heavy cloud, the colour
of smouldering ash,
obscures a misshapen moon.
Tiny fish swarm blackly
on the surface, nudging
crusts from our seafront café.

Suddenly, the wind rises. Trees
sway and open, lights go out
and napkins soar into the air;
waiters leap to catch bottles
and glasses blown off the tables.
A cloud swirls through the streets
and covers our plates with sand.
At once the sea heaves up
a huge, slippery shoulder
against the wall.

In the sudden violence
I see them for the first time:
the small port waiting, still
waiting – nets spread on the wall,
barrels of salt fish on the quay –
and the men who will not return,
but are borne up at a word
as their ship drives through the storm.

DOUGLAS HOUSTON

Funeral in Usk

i.m. *Kenneth McConnan*, obit *17 October 1987*

The chrome-plated trolley with white rubber wheels
Bears the varnished box containing you,
Bumping discreetly between the path's flagstones
Flanked by ornate regularity of trees;
Light saturates their curling brittle leaves.

Were this a casual stroll I should remark
How well the late October chill, noon's brilliance
And colour coincide into rich clarity,
Might photograph it, hoping for results
Worth asking your opinion of,

If burying you were not the matter in hand:
For now the plastic grass is pushed aside
Revealing the narrow void of the shaft
You're lowered into as the vicar intones
To the cautious rhythm of hands that pay out tapes.

This routine function of gravity and space
Frames an unspeakably actual parable
Of birth's reversal, swallowing lyricism
And all evasive sense of other worlds
With sunlight's glint on your vanishing nameplate.

DOUGLAS HOUSTON

Northampton, 1987

for Sam and Iggy

Last Sunday a surreptitious dab of holy water
   On two small foreheads, which surprised you, sons,
My finger dripping from its dip in a receptacle
   That much resembled the bowed ashtrays fixed
To backs of seats upstairs on the old double-decker buses;
   What's that for Dad? – I'll call it superstition
(Than which 'Irreverence is a greater oaf'), to spare me
                                  trying
   To detail a theology of how
Quick gratitude keeps outmanoeuvring inert *non serviam*.
   How both *thank* and *defy* must have an object.

It was one of those high church places where the trappings
                                   rise
   To the occasion of the architecture,
All the air below the ceiling's webbed splendour of vaulting
   Succumbing to the sweet oppression of incense,
The priest trussed in his alb smiling the faithful on their way
   As we came in and headed for the transept
Where works of art, *A. M. D. G.*, by Sutherland and Moore
   Resolved anticipation into attention.
There's Jesus, you said, Ig, approaching the vast cobalt
                            canvas;
   Moore's stone child looked a little bit like you.

Then I went home, a house whose Welsh name means *the*
                           sunny hill,
   Exiled, now voluntarily, from you,
Whose distance is an empty property called *fatherhood*
   That's tenanted on such short holidays;
But to the life I'm glad of here I add more photographs,
   One of you two with Moore's *Madonna and Child*,
Touching its massive base, and touched, perhaps, by the
                               altruism

Of church and art, a moment in your growing
That you might come across one day, upon which I inscribe
Though absent, please infer me from my loves.

LIBBY HOUSTON

Notes on a Meeting

Poised on long feet
and scabby tail,
back arched,
a kept rat, male,
brown, coarse-maned
in his prime,
applies his nose
to my eyelid.
I glimpse his
orange teeth

and hear myself
speak gently
as if to a frightened
child.

TED HUGHES

Kore

What ghosts gather
Over the moonlit grave mounds
Of your breasts?

The common infantry – whose job it is
To cease in approximate numbers
Within the overall event.

What bat-webbed things flitter
About the holy cave
Between your thighs?

The warriors – the selfless ones
Who simply failed to reassemble
From the all-out scrimmage.

Now the shadowy terrace of your lip,
The silent arches of your eyelids
Are their Valhalla.

Are the heroes happy in heaven?

He who wakes
Beside your sleeping face
In the dawn,
And touches you, to make you even more real,
And watches you breathe

He hears the sighs and the sobbings.

PAUL HYLAND

Lament

Lusengo, Zaïre

Ah, mama Ewoyo, you are cold;
There will be buyers for your dried fish
For your smoked monkey, but no seller:
Ah, mama Ewoyo, you are cold.

By my bed a mantis prayed all night
And my sweat flowed like the great river;
By yours, traders spread their hands and wailed:
Ah, mama Ewoyo, you are cold.

At dawn canoes came, fought our bow-wave
To make fast, with *kwanga*, crocodile,
But your stock needs no replenishing:
Ah, mama Ewoyo, you are cold.

Beside a forest village we moored,
Gave money towards your funeral;
A man swung an adze, others dug deep:
Ah, mama Ewoyo, you are cold.

A woman with heavy breasts, grass skirt
Walked round the hole, a soldier watched;
Your raw box borne by many hands:
Ah, mama Ewoyo, you are cold.

At the top of the Congo's great bend
Half a day. Then rattles, chants and prayers
And a spade passed strong arm to strong arm:
Ah, mama Ewoyo, you are cold.

Ah, mama Ewoyo, you are cold;
There will be buyers for your dried fish
For your smoked monkey, but no seller:
Ah, mama Ewoyo, you are cold.

PAUL HYLAND

Wormwood

And the third angel sounded, and there fell a great star from
heaven, burning as it were a lamp . . . And the name of the
star is called wormwood: and the third part of the waters
became wormwood; and many men died of the waters,
because they were made bitter.

Revelation 8: 10–11

This plant belongs to Mars.
It grows on the banks of the Dnieper.
In low potency it cures
nervous tremors, deliriums,
hallucinations, terrors
and poisoning by mushrooms.
Its leaves are grey and downy
and it is bitter.

It blooms in June and July
on waste land in dry regions
and thrives on the banks of the Dnieper.
As *absinthe* it engenders
nervous tremors, deliriums,
hallucinations, terrors,
in excess. In moderation
it is a tonic.

It sends Soviet citizens
back to their bibles,
communists and christians
suffering tremors and terrors,
the bitter text: in Ukrainian
'wormwood' is *Chernobyl*.
Chernobyl on the banks of the Dnieper.
This plant belongs to Mars.

KATHLEEN JAMIE

Poem

'Would Miss Jane Eyre please report to Airport Information.
Miss Jane Eyre, please.' – heard over P.A. at Heathrow.

and he thrust himself into the streams
from every continent – a salmon
shouldering, winding,
searching for a face as pale as chalk.
A bookstore! Surely she'd be there,
peering at the print of worlds she recognized?
No. Nor in the transit lounge,
a satellite to families,
nor the Ladies', weeping beneath
the mounting roar of jets and air conditioning.
He leaps the stairs – she may be taking
a demure, if plastic, cup of tea –
and surveys the concourse. A dark
hooded bird of prey, he sifts, sifts
the dress of all the nations
for a frock in English grey.
Would he catch her tiny voice
in this damned babble?
The information desk – she shakes her head.
'Shall I page again, Sir?'
He gives a brusque 'No. It was an
off-chance, just an off-chance.'
'Is the lady departing or arriving, Sir,
from where?' But he's away,
striding from the terminal,
his landrover nudging the Northbound carriageway.

ELIZABETH JENNINGS

Psalm of Discrepancies

When did I first sing to the clouds of rejection
Turn to the fertile fields with a fiery mind
Set my imagination in tune with storms
Or the wake of storms? I do not know. I know
Only the stretches of memory, the Alps
Of recollection, Himalayas of hope.
Childhood is almost a psalm in itself or a set
Of psalms with their moods of anger and desolation
And hope and imploring. David's language sings me
Back to the shapes of childhood, its squares and oblongs
Its definite colours. I called to the green fields often
Ran through the dew of early morning and gathered
Nosegays and branches for gifts. They were mementoes
For later years, talismans for the ways
No longer straight or certain when clouds are smoky and hide
That joy which swelled beyond my containment, dispersed
Among the green branches of oak and ash and beech.
So I was lost in a world of drama but seldom
Felt lonely or frightened. Never by day I mean,
Never in any resplendent noon. So now
When I am troubled and angry or half-way-between
I turn the pages back in an ancient *Book*
Of Certain Hours and find my childhood markers
Between the pages and all the past is renewed
And dazzles me with the sunrise upon green hills
And sunset over a sea which is not tidal.

ELIZABETH JENNINGS

Tributes

Debts can be burdens and can lead to hate
But there are others which are strong in love
And lift us into a harmonious state,

Judicious, full, compassionate. They move
Us into joys we'd never dreamt about,
Seldom thought possible. I've learnt enough

Of the heart's follies and of serious doubt
To question what the senses claim, I've found
In recent years a warmth which pulls me out

Of lassitude, indifference. Around
The long shelves of my mind I've come upon
Writers, painters, mystics who abound

In gifts my poems have reflected on
And whom I wish to sing and celebrate.
It is not only great stars or the sun

I owe so many debts to. I now state
A poet here, a painter there, a place
That's altered all I do. So I relate

My debts and give back what I've taken, grace.

ELIZABETH JENNINGS

Passion

The violence is over. They lie apart,
They are shapes belonging to no-one or could be
Part of an abstract painting or figure sliding
Upon a Dali sea.
But they are breathing fast still as if they'd been running,
Man and woman, carried by a wind blowing
Out of an open window. Here is passion
Appeased, here is pleasure
Exulted in. And here
Is possible creation. Here could be
Adam and Eve, turning away ashamed.
Here is loss waiting to be redeemed.

JENNY JOSEPH

Generation Gap

'Where have you been, child, that took so long in coming?'
'Curled up in a warm place with the other animals.'

'Why did you not come sooner, while I could play with you?'
'My mother was playing, and had no time for me;

'But you could have seen to the living. They had need of you.
If I were with you now I'd cry and be annoying.
You'd wish for peace again.'

'It is true, my twinkle, my apple of the eye,
That when you are born you will be wet and squally.
And when you are growing I shall worry and complain.
But dreams are fed, my darling, on messy living beings.
It's contrary old people who have no use for pallor:
They want the sun, and comfort and real soft flesh again.

'All that time you kept off when I could have been with you
Were you somewhere gathering merit, becoming beautiful?'

'Curled up in your mind, Grandparent, keeping you
                                        company
And better there, I reckon, than a brat on this bothersome
                                        earth.'

SYLVIA KANTARIS

A Dying Art

When the undertaker visited, I was impressed.
Even his hair was polished black,
and you could tell he was a master craftsman
by his elegiac voice. There is a time and place
for dactyls in the aftermath of even
the most merciful release, as I learned.

Floral tributes and the designated resting-place
were both discussed with reverence before
the sad but necessary topic of the price
of coffins – wood-veneer, polished elm or oak –
was broached, preceded delicately by
a mournfully regretful clearing of the throat.

'They won't want wood-veneer cheap stuff!' my aunt said.
'The choice falls to the nearest and dearest,' he replied,
his pen poised patiently over his notepad.
'May I ask to whom we should address our invoice?'
(You could tell he wished he didn't have to ask.)
He departed with decorum and his first rough draft.

On the day, the ritual was perfect.
We were properly arranged, chief mourners first
behind the hearse, and then the rest in order
of relationship to the deceased. A neighbour
took his cap off as we processed to the church.
Others drew their curtains, as was only right.

The service was a seamless work of art,
as were the bearers – four young funeral apprentices
in matching coats and haircuts (also black).
My London friend was envious, she'd never witnessed
anything so dignified and Hardyesque.
'In town it's just a package-deal,' she said.

The craft requires apprenticeship. Death
needs to be compared with due respect for life.
'What luck to have such treatment as your dad had!'
my friend drooled. 'We'll be lucky if we're bunged into a
ditch.'
'I want that undertaker when I go,' Aunt Lily said.
Me too, or, if he's dead, one of his lads.

GREVEL LINDOP

Contact Lenses

How many times have you dropped on one knee,
a wounded nymph, one hand
cupped at your eye, your hair blown back,
containing tears against the wind,
then staring into your palm
tensed for a moment and caught
like a crystal tear dabbed up
on a fingertip and considered
silently on the tongue,
that lens? Cleared of grit,
the eye gulps it again
and we forget it, except at night
when everything goes *lazy*
as the lenses are put to bed;
or when you lose one, jolted
by a baby's flung fist, a sudden false step
or a missed catch when removing it.

From there the stories begin:
the legendary boyfriend who picked one up on a beach;
that last dogged search when, after midnight,
having turned every soft bear end over end and side
over side with the pressureless delicacy
of a computer-graphics program,
I saw it shining, a pool of love and reassurance
in the desert of fluff and crumbs on the floor of the toybox;
and one we never found, that dropped
on an empty country road we scrutinized
until the quartz and granite chippings and the nubbly tar
between them seemed to pave
my retina but yielded
no blessed gleam until we walked away, leaving cars
or sheep to pulverize the lens as I suppose it lies
today, scattered like the fragments of our
perceptions, where a moment earlier
the humped green and mottled
sheets of mountains had gone weightlessly through,
blowing or silting, a fine crystal dust
under Red Bank and Silver How.

MICHAEL LONGLEY

Marriage

I
I would bring glass flowers to the broken marriages
Because of their flowering time, the once and for all
Hard petals, cups and saucers from a doll's house,
The imaginary roots that grow into the table.

II
The glass iron cooling in your hand will double as
A darning last, a curve of light beneath the holes:
Let me rock along seams with it before your breath
Condenses on the heels and elbows made of glass.

MICHAEL LONGLEY

Cathedral

I
Between the bells and prayers a flower-seller calls
Prices and flower-names the dome translates to echoes,
As though a pigeon had flapped in from the piazza
And perched on the chalice and sipped the sacrament.

II
Because it was dragged on a cart to the cathedral
By untamed calves, the wooden body has emerged
From candle-smoke and incense and, dressed up as God,
Moves through the market to locate those animals.

III
The puppy supposed to suggest a faithful wife
Has nearly nipped her toes for centuries, and begs
To be taken for a walk outside this building
Where stones eat flesh and moonlight eats the stones.

NORMAN MACCAIG

On the North Side of Suilven

The three inch wide streamlet
trickles over its own fingers
down the sandstone slabs
of my favourite mountain.

Like the Amazon, it'll reach the sea.
Like the Volga
it'll forget its own language.

Its water goes down my throat
with a glassy coldness,
like something suddenly remembered.

I drink
its freezing vocabulary
and half understand the purity
of all beginnings.

NORMAN MACCAIG

Old Highland Woman

She sits all day by the fire.
How long is it since she opened the door
and stepped outside, confusing
the scuffling hens and the collie
dreaming of sheep?
Her walking days are over.

She has come here through centuries
of Gaelic labour and loves
and rainy funerals. Her people
are assembled in her bones.
She's their summation. *Before her time*
has almost no meaning.

When neighbours call
she laughs a wicked cackle
with love in it, as she listens
to the sly bristle of gossip,
relishing the life in it,
relishing the malice, with her hands
lying in her lap like holy psalms
that once had a meaning for her, that once
were noble with tunes
she used to sing long ago.

MEDBH MCGUCKIAN

Girl-Mother and Child

Eloquent shadow without soul,
Your arms conceal what is beautiful
Like the loop of the Seine, a position
Of despair; as though keeping still
Were the utmost that could be asked.

That was ten years ago, we are bodies now
That stay up like the moon without
The familiar clues of up and down
Or near and far. You touch ground
With your face alone, one and the same
Autumn field, as if the ground
Were a sky, your fingers skyward.

More important clouds look tossed
And sudden in the sky-replete water
Where your lips were shaped and folded
Till the grain of one outfaced the other:
Your real hand could be living
A half-life of its own somewhere,
Midair, unfurled, rejuvenated.

IAN MCMILLAN

Essential Engineering Works

The train stops somewhere in the lit
midlands, sun reflecting . . . you know
the kind of thing I mean. The lit

midlands. Let me tell you some things
about this poem. This poem happens
on a train stopped in the midlands,

and this poem also happens, if a poem
can happen, in a gallery in Wales,
where a man is looking at photographs.

The two parts of this poem happen at once,
quickly, like the snap of a successful
christmas cracker. I am sorry; this poem

was meant to move more quickly to the
gallery in Wales from the lit midlands.
It is stuck on the line

somewhere between the midlands and Wales.
Listen, you can hear the poem's engine
running. It will start soon, it will

lurch into life. Essential engineering works
are holding this poem still; a man
is standing before a photograph, and he

is seeing only himself in the glass.
Listen, hear the poem's engine running.
Gaze at the photograph and wait, wait.

ROBERT MINHINNICK

Staff

I
Her day-long smile
Welcomes you to the building.
She is money's
Immaculate reflection.

II
The morning ritual
Is to take a steel ruler
And slash her way through envelopes
That do not bear her name.

III
Every minute she connects
One voice to another,
Letting them play
Around each other like finches.
She is the cage.

IV
She hangs the smell of pine-
Forests over enamel,
Plots the orbits of the polisher.
All those nameless good-evenings
Might echo forever
As she flicks on lights in empty corridors.

V
At five in the November dusk
Here is the sum of her day's work,
A corn-coloured sheaf of envelopes
Forgotten long before it's sent
Sliding through the dark.

VI

You remember her from school,
Third form, fourth, a mind
That threatened even then
To fit this flax-blue uniform.
Already there lolls about her face
Compliant middle age,
All the ancestry of discos
And white bread. Her hands
In taking up your purchases
Tap out a brief sonata.

VII

The desks are put back into line,
 A paper with one grey
Footprint swept up.
From the corner there is last retrieved
A broken piece of chalk.
If the board was clean
What would she write?

VIII

Newspaper, sandwich, radio.
She waits with the others
In the revving taxi rank:
As the train pulls out, its passengers
Run to ticketed cars;
And soon the diesel's fainter than the breath
Of her children crumpled
Into balls of sleep.

ROBERT MINHINNICK

Nuns Bathing

From the garden to the dunes
Laughter threads their single file.

Brown as fieldfares
They move towards the waves

And climb the sea-eaten wall
For the green pencils of samphire,

Smiling at something not of this place
And sniffing their lemony fingers.

Each one holds a camera.
Their children are already conceived.

EDWIN MORGAN

Poem

Dear man, my love goes out in waves
and breaks. Whatever is, craves.
Terrible the cage
to see all life from, brilliantly about,
crowds, pavements, cars, or hear the common shout
of goals in a near park.
But now the black bars arc
blue in my breath – split – part –
I'm out – it's art,
it's love, it's rage –

Standing in rage in decent air
will never clear the place of care.
Simply to be
should be enough, in the same city, and let
absurd despair tramp and roar off-set.
Be satisfied with it,
the gravel and the grit,
the struggling eye can't lift,
the veils that drift,
the weird to dree.

Press close to me at midnight as
you say goodbye; that's what it has
to offer, life
I mean. Into the frost with you; into
the bed with me; and get the light out too.
Better to shake unseen
and let real darkness screen
the shadows of the heart,
the vacant part-
ner, husband, wife.

BLAKE MORRISON

Back

A griming of snow along the moortops,
water-beads sissing across the Aga,
sunlight wading through a summer-colt,
the lawn slaphappy after a shower:

before I know it I've descended to this,
a stone rectory lording it in the Pennines,
ringed by horse-chestnuts and a rookery,
near the flush Leeds–Liverpool canal.

You can drop the accent but you never lose
the slang of memory – for belled foxdocks,
the swint-ways chittering of swallows,
the lovely dung-reek of Betty Metcalf's dress.

A long shiver down the back of the land:
even in June it has that chilliness,
wind stevening over the switchbacks,
the water-meadows ruffled then glossy

like the fur down a labrador's spine.
From a far city I keep that place on
for my dream-life, a home to home in on
when I'm alseep or at the brow of it,

heart racing like our drophead Triumph
when we took the canal bridge at West Marton,
our whitewalled tyres as we hit the humpback
treading air for a moment like young lambs.

GRAHAM MORT

Crow Squadron

The sun they flew out of plays
With blacks and blues
In their tattered plumage;
They hang in formation, as if they
Flew into barbed wire and broke
Their wings over its steel barbs:
Their necks tilt, pointing
Their bills at the stake,
At lost targets below.

Flies have blitzed their eyes
Yet their calls – blind
Radio-operators – still spiral
In the dazed, hot air above woods.

The gamekeeper's imperatives
Came smoking from the muzzle of his gun,
Without afterthought:
One moment circling the earth's map,
The next blasted sideways,
Twisting and falling
Into the blurred land.

Their claws still clench this
Sudden mystery,
Their eyes' sockets peer
Into the skull's turret:
Gunner and navigator
Have flown their last mission,
Bluebottles lunch
On last-minute miscalculations
And the bone struts shine.

Above an airstrip of tree-tips,
From the twig hangars of a rookery
Formations float up
Into the quickening currents:
Their cries search the sky,
The earth,
Daylight's retina:
Their hunger pinpoints
Crash-landings from which
The warm lives will spill.

They see the man moving as dust
Upon their eyes' screen:
Only his gun is immortal.

SHEENAGH PUGH

Man getting hammered: between frames

Black hair soaked in sweat,
face flaming, he lights up
one after another: stares
with set eyes at the defeat
inside him. They call this pressure,
he calls it humiliation,
and it isn't over. He must go
out soon, and take some more of it:
smile when it's finished; tell
his tormentor how well he played.
And you could try saying
it's only a game, but he
wouldn't hear you for the hammering
in his head.

PETER REDGROVE

Little Cake

The doctor picks up the metal
Of the afterbirth hammered out
Like bronze in the womb and
Admires its rainbow sheen and
Sniffing it, tucks it away in
His bag; the fluxile metal,
The turquoise, the mother's jade,
The blue-green baggage of the baby.

There is a tie
Of the Old School,
A triple-wound umbilicus,
The tri-via to the twin,
Or the food-line to the molecular library,
Our milliard library in liver-hue binding.

It has an aethyr, this stone,
As the mother has
In the birth-room;
You know the afterbirth has come
By a change of atmosphere,
A trance, like a presence
Entering; the dissolved perfume
Of mother and child and that one
Other dying like a fish
Bloody on a bank:

It is the devoted spectre
Of the betrayed sibling
Mutilated by this birth,
The baby's red luggage, the destroyed twin
Who remains indoors a little longer
Not drinking but bleeding;
The servitor at the round feast,
Called 'placenta' – little cake.

The doctor pops the afterbirth
In his liver-hued bag
Among the turquoise depths
And he brings it with him
To consultations, it assists
His diagnosis like a balsam-root
And the healing images crowd in on him, as:

Almost all
The silver in the world
That is not in the mouths of horses
Or in the cutlery of rich clients
Is dissolved in the seawater,
Is dissolved in the seawater,
That tidal silver-water
Brimmed with the metal of the moon,
Full, when most labours begin.

OLIVER REYNOLDS

Baudelaire's Pipe

I am the pipe of a writer.
The Asian tints congealed
inside my bowl reveal
my master's a heavy smoker.

I'm busiest, a small hookah
bubbling with zeal,
when he's down and he feels
life's dealt him the Joker.

I puff balm,
hazing haloes
of shifting blues

till he's calm,
having taken his cure
from pungent air.

CAROL RUMENS

At the Peter and Paul Fortress

(Leningrad, 4 April 1987)

The prisoners got moved around like tourists
But their demands and ankle-locks were iron.
They hardened in a metamorphosis
Of ultimate conviction not yet on

The Intourist itinerary (not yet
Spelled out), night after dauntless night sat up
Writing the future, dying of what they wrote.
We were their ruined eyes, their stones of hope

– Young brilliance pouring vaguely past, and gone;
The Guide's Komsomol gaze; a daffodil's
Twisted tear; a friendly foreign gun
Home-movieing in the most illustrious cells.

The month is Lenin's. How it laps and glares
Around the spit, blithe as a taxi-ing
Death-boat! Oh Dekabrists, what a spring,
What pointless, blinding life! The Polar Bears*

Are trying to pray for you. They stretch their arms
Along the fortress, tell the frowning sun
How simple flesh is in its naked dreams:
Flesh doesn't lie, nor wish its brother hung.

Faster, faster the prisoners waste their breath
Against the tide. The ice is all in cracks
And streams, the sun defects behind their backs.
A taut throat tells the short rope: Courage! Faith!

---

* members of the Polar Bear Club, devoted to swimming in icy
  conditions

CAROLE SATYAMURTI

Strawberries

I'm spun through time widdershins
to a room lumbered
with a childhood's furniture:
stout mahogany, teak that ousted it,
boxy armchairs, brocatelle
that smartened them as my parents
more or less kept pace with progress
– all there, sharing head-space,
colours mixed by memory to a common brown,

though outside, through French windows,
stand the well-mannered, dusty greens
of a town garden – where I hear
heels clack along the path: my mother
back from a hundred shopping trips
with some treat tucked into her basket;
and where I see my father, the day
he ran to buy me strawberries
and found it was a rag-and-bone man.

As she comes, my vague unease dissolves
– home will be home again;
and, as he does, the wrench
of wishing I could reach into his pocket,
show him the treat he didn't know he'd brought.

JOHN SEWELL

Sunday, His Void Personified

Gale or no gale, out she stormed at 3 a.m.
Roof slates flew after her, chimney bricks
Swept full-lock overhead, met glass somewhere,
Some swinging gate knocked hell out of its frame . . .
Next morning, out of hours, by Hebden's shop,
A glazier, arms outstretched, miming himself
Hoisting something wide from van to waiting frame.
Imagine, how he ran a finger down the sheet's
Cold spine, brought it to an edge, then split it clean.
Now see, he wipes his handiwork away,
To leave – the drab street mirrored on itself,
Or view what's left of yesterday's display –
A consort of shop mannequins, caught in
Flagrante delicto, huffish, disarrayed.

Snakes and Quakes

Anything that wriggles
might be a snake.

Our yard grass whispers
serpentine, stern; seeding
into neighbours' neat gardens.

Coil of cloud returning
with rattling-tail;

the rain a green viper
withdrawing from life,
reclusive in the water table.

Around the new moon,
a snake of light
shakes and

the air cracks its whip;
window glass shatters;
buildings shake and boom.

The snake opens his eye.

Houses, ready to fall,
exhale the scent of him,
that breath of earth.

I sip water,
fearing everything but the snake.

I hold him,
spin in woman circles with him;
his hard drylip against mine,
his tongue mustard,
colour and taste.

He sips my breath.

Doors move suddenly
with no help from hands;
the sky galloping,
rivers zigzagging,
the air's soft growl rippling.

Plumes of trees twist,
green and baffled.

But the serpent is already back
in his secret corner of thin air,
long-necked and unanswerable.

The earth locks its stable doors again.
The horse of quake gone.

I, snake-collared, yawning, garlanded
and sashed with serpents
invisible but coiling and scolloping
electric eel-ishness around me,
watch the golden worm of lightning (my beloved!)
fork his brazen tongue over the black sky,
lisping flame, stammering fire.

KEN SMITH

The Night Whispers

for John and all the men in the world called John

I
There was a friend of mine,
used to offer me a cigarette.
On a Tuesday. John was talking.
He was saying what he hears, his ear
pressed along the wall along the wing.
Time's all there is he says, flat,
to one side, every second word
what he'll never do again with women.
He'll take a light off me though.

He's the man that ate boiled ham raw.
He'll take on a sliced loaf single handed.
Time is the crease in his pants I think,
pressed as in the army under the mattress.
John keeps himself neat. He knows
how quick they'll spirit him away
in a bodybag along the stairs before unlock.
He says he heard the screw say *One Off Sir.*

It's time.

Time he looks back from morning after morning,
his face changing in the same mirror.
Time is the razorblade, the comb's teeth
and the measure of the toothpaste. Time he eats,
shits, drinks, is sometimes merry in,
the fallen grey he lifts off his shoulder.

Time scuffs the shoe and blunts all the nails.
If there were no lights there'd be no fear.
Time I could handle but all this dark stuff
either side between the light and the light.

Time is what.
Time is.

He tells me what he hears in the night whispers
through pipework and brickwork, bars and the hard gloss,
and he writes down the messages: *Oddy's on the roof.*
The nurses are having a party. It's in.
All it costs are little pictures of the Queen.

Oh and love he says. *Love Love Love's*
faint echo on the landings, through the masonry
on a thin late airwave *Love* running down the batteries,
singing on a bent guitar
Lost in the saddle again.

Ah, John.

Lost in time both of us talking about love,
a word born over again and again in the prison house
where so many with their hands killed love,
and then the dark came down forever. So now
behind the yellow wall and the yellow fence
where the wind in a scatter of old leaves
beats the wire to security, the dogs howl
moonward and the champion dopesniffer Duke
sleeps on but John when he sleeps never dreams.

Time is what it is. The protagonist is mad again,
lost in some mean southern border town
all barber shops and bars and far too many shoes.
I've been out again beating my heart on the wind,
and maybe this time John we never get home
and the journey ends here and time's all there is.

The idea is don't die in prison John,
in this part of the nightmare.

II

My brother calls me from the world's other side
and never said which city. He's been robbed,
he's broke, homeless, out of a job and 48,
he's drunk in the wrong house and whose phone is it
and I fear my brother will die in the wind.
He says he's glad dirty money from a dirty job
went to a dirty place to buy a dirty girl junk.
Wherever morning is I hope he'll still be glad.
He'll send an address when he has one.

So now you know the plot. Fox is away
in Australasia waiting for the cops,
and when he called I was thinking about John
and what he tells me: *many things
will never happen.* As for me
I've been too close too long to the damned
and can't leave, lost as are in time,
on my wordtrack covering the territory,
always in the dark thinking I've a lucifer
when I'm far too near the wire when the lights go up
and I'm lost in the saddle again.

Take me home, love, my scars and all my alibis
and my bad manners and whatever wounds we die of.
If you can find me. My name is John.
Maybe you can love what will be left of me.
Take me out of this prison.

PAULINE STAINER

Raking the Japanese Garden

What would Leonardo
have made of it –
the flowing gravel,
the raked spiral,
the unbroken wave against stone?

Here in the monastic garden,
expertise is the zoning
of desire;
enlightenment
the craft of the vanishing-point.

Particulars perfect the ground:
the tilt of rock,
shifting-centre of pebbles,
red lichen an accidental oxide
in the glaze.

In this fugal landscape,
holy conversation
is between circles that never touch,
luminosities
of perilous edge.

Nothing else has ever been
the scarlet persimmons
over the wall,
the parabolas
of their particle chamber,
will not recur.

Intuition is the blade
of the swept vision;
in the overnight snow
the samurai
rinse their swords.

PAULINE STAINER

The Flute Lesson

Today in history of art
we did Roman wallpainting,
studied a frieze of musicians
from Herculaneum;

fluteplayers –
their mouthpieces
still fresh-whittled
from under the hot lava –
master and pupil
fingering the stops.

What caught in my throat
was not their swift embedding –
but how at that last lesson
before my parents knew,
you took the flute from my lips
pressed your mouth to mine
and flutter-tongued.

ANNE STEVENSON

What I miss

is some hexagonal white seal
like a honeycell.
Silence I miss:
the hand on the fiddle
muting the vaulted arrogance
it raises;
the crowded hush
of the conductor's lifted wand,
then the chorale
walking with little empty breaths
through air it praises.

My air is noises
amplified by an ugly pink
barnacle in my ear.
All the music I hear
is a tide dragging pebbles
to and away in my brain.
Sphered, the harmonies fall,
mutate, abort. Emptiness
is like rain
in my insomniac city,
ceaseless and merciless.

R. S. THOMAS

Mass for Hard Times

KYRIE
Because we cannot be clever and honest
and are inventors of things more intricate
than the snowflake – Lord have mercy.

Because we are full of pride
in our humility, and because we believe
in our disbelief – Lord have mercy.

Because we will protect ourselves
from ourselves to the point
of destroying ourselves – Lord have mercy.

And because on the slope to perfection,
when we should be halfway up,
we are halfway down – Lord have mercy.

GLORIA
From the body at its meal's end
and its messmate whose meal is beginning
                                    Gloria.
From the early and late cloud, beautiful and deadly
as the mushrooms we are forbidden to eat
                                    Gloria.
From the stars that are but as dew
and the viruses outnumbering the star clusters
                                    Gloria.
From those waiting at the foot of the helix
for the rope-trick performer to come down
                                    Gloria.
Because you are not there when
I turn, but are in the turning
                                    Gloria.
Because it is not I who look,
but I who am being looked through
                                    Gloria.

Because the captive has found the liberty
that eluded him while he was free
                              Gloria.
Because from the belief that nothing is nothing
it follows that there must be something
                              Gloria.
Because when we count we do not count
the moment between large and small
                              Gloria.
And because, if we are overcome,
we are overcome by nothing
                              Gloria.

CREDO
I believe in God
the Father (Is he married?)
I believe in you the almighty,
who can do anything
you wish. (Forget that irony
of the imponderable.) Rid, therefore,
(if there are not too many
of them) my intestine
of the viruses that against
(in accordance with? Ah, horror!)
your will are in occupation
of its defences. I call
on you, as I have done
often before; (Why repeat,
if he is listening?) to show
you are master of secondary
causation. (What have physics to do
with the heart's need?) Am I
too late, then, with my language?
Are symbols to be in future
the credentials of our approach?
(And how contemporary
is the Cross, that long-bow drawn
against love?) My questions
accumulate in the knowledge
it is words are the kiss of Judas
that must betray you.

94

(My
parentheses are exhausted.) Almighty
pseudonym, grant me at last,
as the token of my belief,
such ability to remain
silent as is the nearest to a reflection
of your silence to which
the human looking-glass may attain.

SANCTUS

The bunsen flame burns and is not consumed,
and the scientist has not removed his shoes
because the ground is not holy.

And because the financiers' sun
is not Blake's sun, there is a
word missing from the dawn chorus.

Yet without subsidies poetry
sings on, celebrating the heart
and the 'holiness of its affections'.

And one listens and must not listen
in vain for the not too clinical
sanctus that is as the halo of its transplanting.

BENEDICTUS

Blessed be the starved womb
and the replete womb.

Blessed the slug in the dew
and the butterfly among the ash-cans.

Blessed be the mind that brings forth good and bad
and the hand that exonerates it.

Blessed be the adder among its jewels
and the child ignorant of how love must pay.

Blessed the hare who, in a round
world, keeps the tortoise in sight.

Blessed the cross warning: No through road;
and that other cross with its arm out, pointing both ways.

Blessed the woman who is amused
at Adam feeling for his lost rib.

Blessed the clock with its hands over its face
pretending it is mid-day, when it is mid-night.

Blessed be the far side of the Cross and the back
of the mirror that they are concealed from us.

AGNUS DEI
No longer the Lamb
but the idea of it.
Can an idea bleed?
On what altar
does one sacrifice an idea?

It gave its life
for the world? No,
it is we give our life
for the idea that nourishes
itself on the dust in our veins.

God is love. Where
there is no love, no God?
There is only the gap between
word and deed we try
narrowing with an idea.

CHARLES TOMLINSON

The House in the Quarry

What is it doing there, this house in the quarry?
   On the scrap of a height it stands its ground:
The cut-away cliffs rise round it
   And the dust lies heavy along its sills.
Still lived in? It must be, with the care
   They have taken to train its vine
Whose dusty pergola keeps back the blaze
   From a square of garden. Can it be melons
They are growing, a table someone has set out there
   As though, come evening, you might even sit at it
Drinking wine? What dusty grapes
   Will those writhen vine-stocks show for the rain
To cleanse in autumn? And will they taste then
   Of the lime-dust of this towering waste,
Or have transmuted it to some sweetness unforeseen
   That original cleanliness could never reach
Rounding to insipidity? All things
   Seem possible in this unreal light –
The poem still to be quarried here,
   The house itself lit up to repossess
Its stolen site, as the evening matches
   Quiet to the slowly receding thunder of the last
Of the lorries trundling the unshaped marble down and past.

ROBERT WELLS

Middle Age

The temples, lakes and islands; rooms and roads:
When we go wandering, soon there's too much
To gather into consequence. Our touch
Has brushed too many stones; too many gods
Have played the host to us and had their claim
Shrugged off. Old pockets, worn-out wallets keep
The bills and tickets. In a drawer, a heap
Of shells recalls a place, perhaps a name.

Youth's body, like a broken statue, lies
Deep-buried with the meaning that it gave.
We cast about for something we can save
By which to save ourselves; more blank than wise
For all the miles that brought us to this ground,
Still ignorant of where value can be found.

VAL WARNER

Bottled Moon

A packet, slipping down the oceanic deliquescence . . .

Once in a blue moon, I'd broach that envelope,
plundering that kangaroo pouch of the past, flip

through papers, aged by dead suns beyond
their age, after some legal document, only meaning-
ful *in absentia*. God knows how it came
there, your Ernst card growing blue

gentians and olives between gilded typescript
sheets. There, a baby-face and drink-ruddy moon glares on
a post-Armstrong moonscape, the landscape
of our common form, slitheringly over-

lapping . . . under the belljar of the night, pickled

strange fruit. Shades of Lady
Day. The message in the bottle on the moon-

tied tide sings 'Why don't we meet sometime
if you like?', signed only by your hand
on a Tate postcard, franked in Dover.

HILARY LLEWELLYN WILLIAMS

The Bee-Flight

That was a strange, rare place, in a loop
between river and nippled hill
with a crooked sandstone church and trees
that corkscrewed, and a massive leaning yew
one thousand years thick, peeled rosy flesh
and a woman carved into the north wall
with legs agape, and a man with a bird's head
whistling sorcery. The ground rose
in hummocks: the past, carelessly buried,
trying to break through. Snowdrops showed white
and wet below the mound. I stood at the cusp
of spring in a flayed landscape
bleached-out by frost, stripped clean

as an old bone, sucked dry. I'd thought
there was nothing to fill me, nothing to speak to me;
but here was rain smelling of turned earth,
the sun in watercolour, curved paths,
storybook trees, bark swirled, bulged-out and fissured
peopling the place. At the edge of a pool
a straddled oak with a hole at eye
level, forced me to stare. Birds calling, then
a humming past my ear, and again: brown bees
sailing in from the sedges, dipping down
into darkness, hollow mouth-oak, in and in
with grains of new gold. A ragged shower blew
up from the west. Something unfolding, stirring

under my feet. The lumpy, breast-topped crag
now spiralled in light; the bird-man suddenly answered
by choruses of wings, and the opened thighs
of the sandstone witch by the presence of flying bees.